SAMUEL F. B. *Morse*

SPIRIT
of America®

Samuel F. B. *Morse*

INVENTOR AND CODE CREATOR

By Judy Alter

The Child's World®
Chanhassen, Minnesota

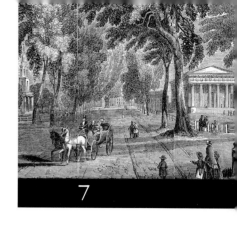
7

SAMUEL F. B. *Morse*

Published in the United States of America by The Child's World®
PO Box 326 • Chanhassen, MN 55317-0326 • 800-599-READ • www.childsworld.com

Acknowledgments
The Child's World®: Mary Berendes, Publishing Director

Editorial Directions, Inc.: E. Russell Primm, Emily J. Dolbear, and Pam Rosenberg, Editors; Dawn Friedman, Photo Researcher; Linda S. Koutris, Photo Selector; Sarah E. De Capua, Copy Editor; Susan Ashley, Proofreader; Tim Griffin, Indexer

Photo
Cover: Hulton Archive/Getty Images; National Portrait Gallery, Smithsonian Institution/Art Resource, NY: 8; Smithsonian American Art Museum, Washington, DC/Art Resource, NY: 11; Corbis: 7, 27; Bettmann/Corbis: 9, 10, 12, 22, 23; Francis G. Mayer/Corbis: 13; Hulton-Deutsch Collection/Corbis: 21; The Granger Collection, New York: 18, 25; Hulton Archive/Getty Images: 2, 6, 14, 15, 28; North Wind Picture Archives: 19, 20, 26; Smithsonian American Art Museum, Transfer from U.S. Capitol: 17.

Library of Congress Cataloging-in-Publication Data
Alter, Judy, 1938–
  Samuel F. B. Morse : inventor and code creator / by Judy Alter.
    p. cm.
"Spirit of America."
Summary: A biography of the artist and inventor who devised the world's
first practical telegraph system.
Includes bibliographical references and index.
  ISBN 1-56766-446-6 (Library bound : alk. paper)
  1. Morse, Samuel Finley Breese, 1791–1872—Juvenile literature. 2. Inventors—
United States—Biography—Juvenile literature. 3. Artists—United States—Biography—
Juvenile literature. 4. Telegraph—Juvenile literature. 5. Morse code—Juvenile literature. [1.
Morse, Samuel Finley Breese, 1791–1872. 2. Inventors. 3. Artists.] I. Title.
  TK5243.M7I58 2003
  621.383'092—dc21

2002151666

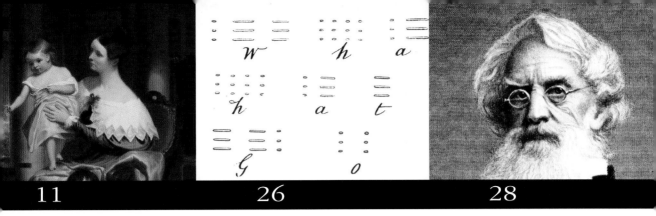

Contents

Chapter ONE

A Rebellious Youth

SAMUEL MORSE WAS AN ARTIST, A PHOTOGRAPHER, an inventor, a politician, and a businessman. He is best known for developing the **telegraph** and Morse **code**.

In the early 1830s, Morse became interested in communicating instantly over long distances. When he went to Europe, he wanted to let his mother know he had arrived safely. The letter he wrote to her took a month to arrive. When Morse's first wife died suddenly, he did not get the message for six days. He missed his own wife's funeral!

Morse knew that instant communication would be important to the entire world. He worked for 12 years to send his first telegraph message.

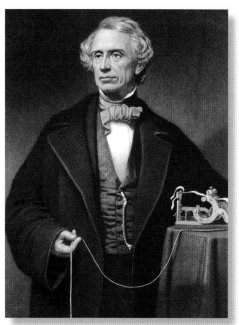

Samuel Morse with his telegraph

Samuel Morse's full name was Samuel Finley Breese Morse. He was born on April 27, 1791, in Charlestown, Massachusetts. His father was Jedidiah Morse, a preacher and author of geography books. His mother was the granddaughter of a past president of Princeton University in New Jersey.

Morse attended Yale College.

Samuel's parents called him Finley. They expected him to have great success in life. Samuel Morse's parents had 11 children, but only three boys survived. His younger brothers were Sidney and Richard.

As a boy, Samuel had many interests. He started projects but didn't always finish them. One of his favorite activities was drawing. He began school at Phillips Academy in Andover, Massachusetts, when he was seven years old. He was not a great student. Sometimes he spent his study time drawing pictures.

In 1805, at the age of 14, he entered Yale College (present-day Yale University) in Connecticut. He still did not study much,

Interesting Fact

▶ Morse's first telegraph, built in 1837, used a home-made battery and gears from an old clock. It produced a line on paper ribbon called ticker tape. The dips in the line had to be translated into letters.

John Singleton Copley was a very famous American artist.

although he liked chemistry and lectures about electricity. When not attending classes, Samuel liked hunting and ice-skating. He also drew pictures of his classmates and sold them for spending money. This activity helped him decide to be an artist.

Morse graduated from Yale in 1810, when art was still new in America. People who wanted to study art had to go to Europe. Morse's parents could not afford to send him to Europe. Besides, they did not think he could make a living as an artist. They wanted him to go home to Massachusetts and work for a bookseller. Morse did as they wished. In the evenings, he painted.

Samuel Morse showed his work to John Singleton Copley, a successful American artist. Washington Allston also looked at Morse's work. Allston was an American who had studied in England. The two artists were convinced Morse had talent. They helped convince his parents to send him to England to study with Benjamin West. West was a famous American artist who lived in England. Samuel "Finley" Morse sailed for England on July 15, 1811.

FOR HUNDREDS OF YEARS, THE ONLY way to send a message was to write it down and give it to a messenger to deliver. Messengers usually rode horseback. Thousands of years ago, Roman and Greek messengers ran on foot.

The invention of the telescope sped up communication. Men mounted messages on huge boards. They were read from a distance, through a telescope. Then one reader mounted the message on his board for the next reader. The boards had to be within sight of each other, so each did not cover a great distance. They could not be used at night or if the weather was foggy.

In 1792, a Frenchman named Claude Chappe invented the semaphore telegram. Platforms 15 miles (24 kilometers) apart held tall poles with jointed arms that moved in many directions. The position of the arms communicated the message to the viewer.

Semaphore flags have also been used to transmit messages. The sender holds a flag in each hand and makes a letter of the alphabet by moving the flags into different positions, ranging from straight up to straight down.

Today, we communicate instantly through the Internet, the fax, and the telephone. Samuel Morse would have been amazed by these inventions.

Chapter TWO

An Artistic Career

MORSE WAS A SUCCESSFUL ART STUDENT, BUT he was impatient. He expected instant riches and fame. Morse was given a statue of **Hercules**. West wanted Morse to draw the statue. Morse thought it was a dumb assignment. Then he realized that he was learning **anatomy** as he drew. The finished drawing won him a place in the Royal Academy of Arts in London. In 1812, he won a gold medal from an art society for his clay model of the statue. Morse later did a painting called *Dying Hercules.*

People viewing paintings inside the Royal Academy of Arts in London

In 1815, Morse's parents called him home. They could not afford to pay for his education in Europe any longer. They didn't think Americans would buy the kinds of paintings Morse was doing. They did believe, however, that Americans would buy paintings of themselves. So they encouraged him to paint portraits.

Goldfish Bowl, *a painting by Samuel Morse*

Morse returned to the United States and became a **tramp** painter. He traveled from small town to small town trying to sell portraits. He hoped to earn $50 for each portrait. Instead, he earned $15 dollars for each. Few people wanted their portraits

A portrait of John Adams painted by Morse

painted. Still fewer could afford to pay $50 for one, which was a lot of money in the early 1800s.

In 1818, Samuel Morse married Lucretia Walker. They had three children—Susan, Charles, and Finley. Morse still traveled to sell his portraits. He and Lucretia dreamed of the day he could support their family by doing historical paintings, which he enjoyed doing more than portraits. Creating portraits was difficult. The people being painted always wanted Morse to change their nose or hair or eyes.

In 1819, Morse painted a portrait of U.S. president James Monroe. In 1822, he completed *The House of Representatives,* a painting of the members of the U.S. House of Representatives. In 1825, he was called to Washington, D.C., to paint a portrait of General Marquis de Lafayette, a hero of the American Revolution (1775–1783). Morse's fame was growing. He would soon be able to buy Lucretia a new house. While in Washington, he received news that Lucretia had died suddenly.

Morse was lonely and heartbroken. He was finally successful, but it meant nothing without Lucretia. He moved to New York, painted portraits, and helped to start the National Academy of Design. The academy offered young artists training in painting, architecture, and engraving. Morse eventually sold everything, left his children with relatives, and returned to Europe. He was gone for three years.

In 1832, on his return voyage to America, Morse heard passengers talking

Morse painted this portrait of Lafayette in 1825.

about electromagnetism, an electric force that causes something to act like a magnet. Someone said that electricity could travel in an instant over electric wire of any length. This idea caught Morse's imagination.

A horseshoe-shaped electromagnet used by English physicist and chemist Michael Faraday

Morse knew that he could make electricity with a battery and send it through wire. If he could start and stop the electricity, the same thing would happen anywhere along the wire. An **electromagnet** would stop and start the electric signal. He would make a code to stand for the letters of the alphabet by starting and stopping the electrical current. When he returned to America, Morse spent all his time on this new project.

The parts of an early electromagnetic device

15

THERE IS A STORY TOLD ABOUT HOW SAMUEL MORSE THOUGHT HE COULD FINISH his drawing, *Dying Hercules*, in a couple of days. He showed the completed work to Benjamin West (right). West said, "Fine. Now finish it." Morse said that it was finished. West showed him where it needed work and said it should take another week to finish. Morse spent two more weeks on the drawing before he showed it to Benjamin West.

West studied the drawing for a long time. He said it was excellent. Then he said, "Go on and finish it." Morse again said that it was finished. West pointed out problems with the work. Morse thought it would take another week to follow his teacher's suggestions. He had always been in a hurry to move on to the next project. Now he was spending three weeks on one drawing.

When Morse took the drawing back to West after another week, West told him once again to finish it. Morse worked on it, but he was tired and discouraged. When he took it back to West for the fourth time, West once more told him to finish it. Morse said he could not. He had done the best he could.

West told him then that he had learned more from that one project than he would have learned from many half-finished drawings. The half-finished drawings would not be good enough to get him into the Royal Academy of Art. The drawing that had taken him more than four weeks to complete won him a place at that school.

17

Chapter THREE

The Inventor's Struggle

Alfred Vail was one of Morse's students.

BACK IN NEW YORK, MORSE HAD NO MONEY. His brothers gave him a work space in the attic of their newspaper building. Then he was offered a position as professor of painting and sculpture at New York University.

The salary was small. He lived in his classroom. Sometimes his students brought him supper.

Leonard Gale was a scientist who taught at the university. He believed in Morse's telegraph project. So did a student named Alfred Vail. Vail's father helped to pay for Morse's work.

Morse thought he could earn enough money painting to pay for his telegraph project. He was very busy, however. He had to study his students' work and discuss it with them, as West had done for him. At night, he worked on his telegraph. He built his first telegraph with a picture frame, a table, and pieces of lead. He did not have much time for painting.

For years, Morse had hoped to be asked to do one of the four paintings that would go in the **rotunda** of the new U.S Capitol in Washington, D.C. Morse needed money. He hoped the project would help him earn what he needed. John Quincy Adams was in charge of the committee to choose the artists. Adams liked European artists better than American artists. Morse was not chosen. This experience ended his career as an artist.

Morse once again turned his attention to the telegraph project. He spent his days putting pieces of wire together and wrapping them in cotton. Today, wire comes in huge rolls and is **insulated** in plastic. In the early 1800s, it came in short pieces and was not insulated. He also worked out his code, changing it several times.

The rotunda of the U.S. Capitol

At that time, many Americans knew that scientists had been experimenting with electricity for years. Few Americans, however, expected it to be useful for anything. Morse strung wire around his university classroom and invited well-known businessmen to see how his telegraph worked. The men were impressed, but they didn't think the device was useful. None of them gave Morse money to continue his project.

Morse was asked to demonstrate his telegraph to many leaders of government and business.

Morse showed the telegraph to the U.S. president, members of Congress, and other government leaders. They found it interesting, but Congress did not vote to give him any money. Morse traveled to Europe to raise money but that, too, was unsuccessful. To support himself, Morse gave painting lessons and took photographs. It was the telegraph, however, that held his interest.

In 1842, he and Gale arranged to show the telegraph to the public. They laid two miles (3.2 km) of wire

Morse went to Washington, D.C., to ask Congress to give him money for his telegraph project.

across New York harbor. An operator would be on either side of the harbor. Businessmen were invited, too. At first, the telegraph worked. Then it went silent. People laughed and called Morse a **fraud**. Later he learned that a ship in the harbor had pulled up the cable onto its deck. Not knowing what it was, the crew cut it and threw it back in the water.

Morse's only hope was getting money from Congress. He went to Washington in December 1842. He stayed until March 1843. The House of Representatives voted to give money to Morse for his telegraph project. However, the Senate still had to agree to give Morse the money.

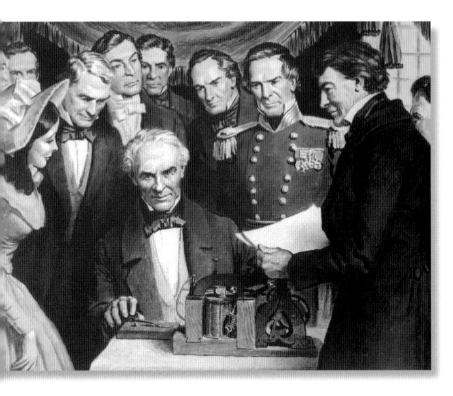

Morse (seated) sends the first telegraph message with Annie Ellsworth (far left) looking on.

In early March, the Senate was getting ready to adjourn, or stop work for a period of time. On the last night the Senate met, Morse waited late into the night for the members to vote. Discouraged, he went back to the boardinghouse where he had been staying. He believed he would never get the money he needed from Congress. He decided to pack his belongings and leave Washington the next day.

The following morning, Morse came down from his boardinghouse room. The young daughter of a friend was waiting. Annie Ellsworth asked if she was the first to tell him the news. He didn't know what she meant. She told him that the Senate had voted to give him $30,000! Morse was overjoyed and began work at once. He told young Annie that she could choose the words for the first message he would send.

MORSE CODE TRANSLATES THE ENGLISH ALPHABET INTO A SERIES OF dots and dashes. Each letter is assigned a pattern of dots and dashes. People who send messages by code do not use the words "dot" and "dash." The terms are "dit" and "dah." The "t" in "dit" is silent unless it is the last letter in the word. The most familiar Morse code message is SOS, the request for help or rescue. An S is three dots. An O is three dashes. In Morse code it is di-di-di dah-dah-dah di-di-dit. It looks like this:

● ● ● — — — ● ● ●.

Morse code messages can be sent other ways than by telegraph. Messages can be written on paper, tapped with fingers or a pencil, flashed with a flashlight, or even blinked with the eyelids. All of this takes practice. It is easier to learn the code by listening to it. It's difficult to memorize the way the letters look. You can find books about learning Morse code in the library or at bookstores.

Chapter FOUR

Success!

Interesting Fact

▸ Morse ran for mayor of New York City twice. He lost both times.

MORSE AND HIS PARTNERS, LEONARD GALE and Alfred Vail, had only two months to lay insulated wire between Washington, D.C., and Baltimore, Maryland, a distance of more than 35 miles (56.3 km). When the deadline was almost upon them, Morse ran a test. The telegraph did not work. He didn't know where the trouble was. It could be in the batteries that supplied the power. It could be in the cable.

A man named Ezra Cornell used a team of mules and a plow to dig the trench. Then he laid the cable in the trench and covered it. As the day neared to show the telegraph to Congress, however, the plow crashed into a huge rock and broke into pieces. Morse had to wait for the plow to be rebuilt. He used

that time to figure out why the telegraph wasn't working.

Morse and his helpers dug up the
cable. They found the trouble. In
many places the insulation—the
covering that kept the wire from
touching other objects that conduct
electricity—was burned. This left the
wire exposed. Trying to send electricity through it was like sending water
through a leaky pipe.

Morse had spent $20,000 so far.
Now he would have to start all over
again. He knew he wouldn't be ready
in time to show the telegraph to
Congress. He reread the stack of notes he
had taken about telegraphs. He discovered
the idea that an overhead wire could be used
instead of an underground cable. It could be
strung on poles 30 feet (9.2 meters) high.
The wire would only have to be insulated
where it touched the poles.

Ezra Cornell had an idea for insulating
the wire where it touched the poles. He
suggested glass knobs, like those on dresser
drawers. Morse decided to use them.

*Morse discovered that it was
better to string the telegraph
wire from poles than to
bury it underground.*

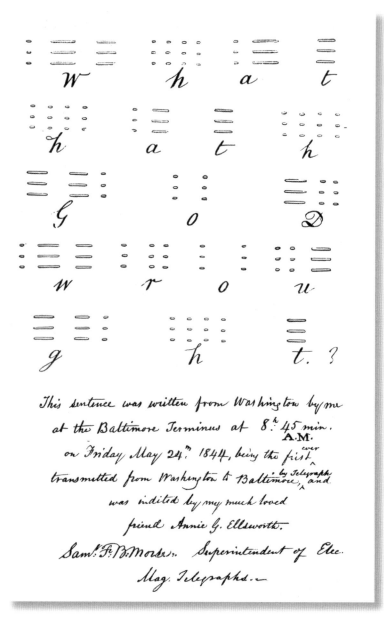

What hath God wrought?

This sentence was written from Washington by me at the Baltimore Terminus at 8.ʰ 45 min. A.M. on Friday, May 24.ᵗʰ 1844, being the first ever transmitted from Washington to Baltimore, by Telegraph, and was indited by my much loved friend Annie G. Ellsworth.

Samˡ. F. B. Morse. Superintendent of Elec. Mag. Telegraphs.—

The first telegraph message was sent on Friday, May 24, 1844.

On May 24, 1844, Morse sat in a room inside the U.S. Capitol in Washington, D.C. Annie Ellsworth was there, too, holding a piece of paper. On it was written the message he had promised her she could choose. Her mother helped her pick out a verse from the Bible, Numbers 23:23. Morse told her it was a good choice.

Alfred Vail was in a room in Baltimore. Morse told his audience that he would send Vail the message. When it was received, Vail would send it back, so that it was recorded in Washington and in Baltimore. With a series of dots and dashes, Morse sent the message:

"What hath God wrought!"—which means "See what God has done!" Within one minute, the message had gone to Baltimore and come back. His audience was amazed.

By 1846, companies had used Morse's **patent** to build telegraph lines from Washington, D.C., to Buffalo, New York, and Boston, Massachusetts. By 1853, there were 23,000 miles (37,007 km) of telegraph wires in the United States. In 1868, cable was laid across the Atlantic Ocean. Soon the whole world knew Morse code.

The remainder of Morse's life was much happier than the period when he struggled to develop the telegraph. He made money from the telegraph. In 1847, he bought Locust Grove, an estate in New York's Hudson River valley. Morse brought his children to live there with him. In 1848, at the age of 57, he married Sarah Griswold. They had several more children.

Laying telegraph cable under the Atlantic Ocean allowed messages to be sent from North America to Europe.

▶ Samuel F. B. Morse is buried in Greenwood Cemetery in Brooklyn, New York.

Samuel Morse was given many awards in honor of his invention of the telegraph.

Morse received many awards for his work. He was honored by the countries of Turkey, Prussia (present-day Germany), Austria, France, Denmark, and Spain. He was praised at banquets in London, Paris, and New York. The governments of many countries gave him a lot of money. One of his most important honors was the creation of a statue of him that was put in New York City's Central Park on June 10, 1871.

In his later years, Morse was a wealthy man. He gave generously to the National Academy of Design and to several colleges, including Yale. He also shared his money with charities and poor artists.

Samuel F. B. Morse died of pneumonia in New York City on April 2, 1872. He was 80 years old. Morse did not invent the telegraph alone. Others had been working on similar projects before he did, but he was the first to make it work. He fully deserves to have the telegraphic code bear his name.

1791　Samuel Morse is born on April 27 in Charlestown, Massachusetts.

1799　Morse attends Phillips Academy.

1810　Morse graduates from Yale College.

1811　He sails to Europe to study painting.

1815　Morse returns to the United States.

1818　Samuel Morse marries Lucretia Walker.

1825　Lucretia Morse dies. The National Academy of Design is started with Morse's help.

1829　Morse returns to Europe.

1832　Morse sails back to America and is offered a job as a professor of of painting and sculpture at the New York University.

1835　Morse sends a one-way electric communication over a half-mile (nearly 1 km) distance.

1838　He travels to Europe to seek money to pay for his telegraph project.

1843　The U.S. Congress awards Morse $30,000 for his telegraph project.

1844　The first long-distance telegraph message is sent from Washington, D.C., to Baltimore, Maryland.

1847　Morse buys the Locust Grove estate in New York's Hudson River valley.

1848　Morse marries Sarah Griswold.

1871　A statue of Morse is placed in New York City's Central Park on June 10.

1872　Morse dies on April 2 in New York.

anatomy (uh-NAT-uh-mee)
Anatomy is the structure of a plant or animal. Morse learned about the anatomy of the human body when he studied art.

code (KOHD)
A code is a system in which sounds or symbols are used to send messages. Samuel Morse developed a code for sending messages by telegraph.

electromagnet (i-lek-troh-MAG-nit)
An electromagnet is a magnet that becomes stronger when electricity passes through it. A telegraph uses an electromagnet to send messages.

fraud (FRAHD)
A fraud is someone who tries to cheat or trick others. Samuel Morse was called a fraud when it appeared that his telegraph didn't work.

Hercules (HER-kyuh-leez)
In Greek mythology, Hercules was a hero of unusual strength. Morse's drawing of Hercules won him a place at the Royal Academy of Arts in London.

insulated (IN-suh-late-ed)
Something that is insulated is covered by material that does not conduct electricity, sound, or heat. Wire that is used to carry electricity is insulated.

patent (PAT-nt)
A patent is document that says a certain person or company is the only one with the right to make or sell an invention for a certain number of years. Morse received a patent from the U.S. government for the telegraph.

rotunda (roh-TUHN-duh)
A rotunda is a round building or hall that is usually covered with a dome. The U.S. Capitol in Washington, D.C., has a large rotunda.

telegraph (TEL-uh-graf)
A telegraph is a device or system for sending messages over long distances. It uses a code of electrical signals sent by wire.

tramp (TRAMP)
A tramp is someone who travels from town to town on foot, often begging for food or work. Morse was a tramp painter who went from town to town searching for work painting portraits.

For Further INFORMATION

Web Sites

Visit our homepage for lots of links about Samuel F. B. Morse and Morse code:
http://www.childsworld.com/links.html

Note to Parents, Teachers, and Librarians:
We routinely verify our Web links to make sure they're safe,
active sites—so encourage your readers to check them out!

Books

Hossell, Karen Price. *Morse Code.* Chicago: Heinemann Library, 2002.

Latham, Jean Lee. *Samuel F. B. Morse: Artist-Inventor.* New York: Chelsea House, 1991.

Parker, Janice. *Messengers, Morse Code & Modems.* Austin: Raintree/Steck-Vaughn, 2000.

Tiner, John Hudson, and Shirley Young (illustrator). *Samuel Morse: Artist with a Message.* Milford, Mich.: Mott Media, 1987.

.

Places to Visit or Contact

Locust Grove
To see the home where Morse lived in his later years
2683 South Road
Poughkeepsie, NY 12601
845/454-4500

National Museum of American History
Smithsonian Institution
To see the exhibit Information Age: People, Information & Society
14th Street and Constitution Avenue, N.W.
Washington, DC 20013-7012
202/357-2700

Index